The love of Christ revives love wherever we think that the ability to love has been lost.

At a time when our world is facing threats from all sides—wars in many places that show signs of escalation, dangerous changes to the climate that are already causing irreversible damage to the quality of life for many, and increasingly violent rifts between domestic factions—Pope Francis has chosen to release an encyclical, *Dilexit nos* (He Loved Us), to remind us of the unconditional and never-failing love of Christ for all of us.

When we open ourselves to this love, he says, we can become the ambassadors of Christ that we are called to be by our baptism, and we can help change our own hearts as well as the hearts of others.

May these thirty reflections, based on the words of *Dilexit nos*, inspire you to open yourself to the love of Christ, which is ready and willing to embrace you!

The quotes (at times paraphrased) from
Pope Francis that open each reflection
were chosen by Deborah McCann,
who also wrote the reflections and the
"Ponder" and "Pray" pieces.

Second printing 2025

Copyright © 2024 **TWENTY-THIRD PUBLICATIONS**,
a division of Bayard; 977 Hartford Turnpike Unit A, Waterford, CT 06385;
860-437-3012 or 800-321-0411; twentythirdpublications.com.

No part of this publication may be reproduced in any manner without
prior written permission of the publisher. All rights reserved.

Cover image: © zatletic - stock.adobe.com

ISBN: 978-1-62785-839-7 ■ Printed in the U.S.A.

1 | PAUSING TO REFLECT

We all need to rediscover the importance of the heart.

We live, says Pope Francis, in a world of frenetic speed, dizzying complexity, and so much noise from all sides that it's impossible to find quiet space just to gather our thoughts. We're constantly at the mercy of marketing campaigns designed to make us consume ever more things that we don't really need and that don't satisfy us once we have them.

The pope reminds us that the heart has long been a symbol for the love of Christ—especially the image of the Sacred Heart. When we take time to be still within ourselves, we can rediscover the love that is waiting for us.

PONDER

What one distraction in my life can I remove today to make room to heed God's voice?

PRAY

God of love and goodness, open my heart to accept yours.

2 | START BY LOOKING WITHIN

*Instead of chasing the superficial
and playing a role for the benefit of others,
think about the really important questions in life.*

Pope Francis suggests that we take time to consider life's deepest questions: Who am I? Who am I for others? Who am I for God? At the end of my life, how have I treated others, and how have I treated myself? All these questions, the pope says, lead back to the heart. We find God's love when we remember that God is present with us. Then we can peel back the superficialities that often shield us from seeing who we really are.

PONDER

Have I pondered whether God finds in me someone worthy of love?

PRAY

God of love and goodness, shine your light of love in my heart!

3 | THE HEART'S MESSAGE

If we fail to appreciate the unique message of the heart, we miss the messages that the mind alone cannot communicate.

When we find ourselves consumed by the busyness and noise of everyday life—as compelling as our tasks and responsibilities may be—we lose sight of the mystery and beauty of the part of us that rests with God. Pope Francis says, "If we devalue the heart, we also devalue what it means to speak from the heart, to act with the heart, to cultivate and heal the heart." We miss out on the richness of our encounters with others. Most of all, we lose our sense of our personal history of loving, which is all that will matter in the end.

PONDER
When was the last time I took a good, deep look at myself?

PRAY
God of love and goodness, open my eyes to see how interconnected we are!

4 | THE HEART AS "GUEST HOUSE"

All authentic bonding begins with the heart, since a relationship not shaped by the heart cannot overcome the fragmentation of individualism.

"A society dominated by narcissism and self-centeredness," says Pope Francis, "will increasingly become 'heartless.'" We need to rediscover the peaceful wholeness of the heart, which is the root of our experience of love. When we are self-centered we can't relate on a real level with others, nor can we truly relate to God. The pope says that in order to be open to God, we have to build God a welcoming place—a "guest house" in our heart.

PONDER

How much space do I have in my heart for God?

PRAY

God of love and goodness, help me to create and maintain a space for you always in my heart.

5 | WHERE EVERYTHING MAKES SENSE

The heart is the place where everything can make sense.

Pope Francis uses the example of the Blessed Mother, who "kept" and "pondered" things in her heart. We too keep in our heart all the mysteries of our life, the things we have experienced or seen or heard that we do not fully understand. We keep and ponder them in the heart until they make sense. Mary was able to do this, he says, because she was open to God and trusted in God's love for her. When we are open to God and trust in God's love for us, we too can take time to stop and reflect on how God is speaking to us.

PONDER
Is there something nagging at my brain that my heart might solve if I take the time to let it?

PRAY
God of love and goodness, please give me the patience to let my heart do its work.

6 | THE CORE OF OUR BEING

If love reigns in our heart, we become the persons we are meant to be. Every human being is created above all else for love.

"In the deepest fiber of our being," Pope Francis says, "we were made to love and to be loved." He points out that the heart is our very core—where the body, mind, and soul all come together to be the person God has created us to be. We are here to do something unique in God's plan. When we take time to listen to what God is saying in our heart, we can discover how God's love can become visible through us and shared with everyone.

PONDER

If I listened carefully to what God is telling me, are there people in my life to whom I should be showing God's love?

PRAY

God of love and goodness, fill my heart with your love so that I may share it unselfishly with others.

7 | LIVING IN LOVE

When we contemplate the meaning of our lives, perhaps the most decisive question is, "Do I have a heart?"

We've all had those moments when we come to grips with who exactly we are—what our purpose is. Pope Francis says those are the moments when we need to realize that love is our driving force. That's when we come closest to truth, to sensing things coming into place. As Pope Francis says, "Everything comes together in a state of coherence and harmony." When we take the time to discover the heart that is the core of our being, we come face to face with love, the divine force that lives in us always.

PONDER
Do I make an effort every day to center myself in love?

PRAY
God of love and goodness, help me to live in your love.

8 | DISCOVERING THE HEART OF CHRIST

In the heart of Christ, we truly come at last to know ourselves, and we learn how to love.

Pope Francis stresses that we do not discover this heart of Christ by our abilities alone, but by centering ourselves in the Sacred Heart, "that core of his being, which is a blazing furnace of divine and human love and the most sublime fulfillment to which humanity can aspire." That is where we truly find ourselves and learn how to love. This often runs counter to the message of how the world champions self-realization or success—all the more reason to put ourselves in Christ's hands.

PONDER
Do I stand in my own way in trying to get closer to God?

PRAY
God of love and goodness, help me to set aside distractions that keep me from placing my life in your hands.

9 | HOW JESUS WORKS—STILL!

Jesus shows that God is closeness, compassion, and tender love.

Pope Francis points out that if we look at the gospels, it is clear that Jesus never worked at a distance from people. Rather, he always approached them on a very personal level, not judging or condemning, but always reaching out with the deepest understanding and love. This is how we are to follow his example—by being ready to love our neighbor, whomever that might be, to be always open to the encounter with another. It can be hard to reach out so openly, but Christ, through the Spirit, will give us the grace.

PONDER

When have I shied away from encounters with others? How might I open myself more freely?

PRAY

God of love and goodness, give me courage and strength so that I might share your love and compassion wherever it's needed.

10 | OPENING UP TO ENCOUNTER CHRIST

Jesus will always find a way to be present in your life, so that you can encounter him.

Jesus didn't stop reaching out to others after his passion, death, and resurrection. Indeed, Pope Francis assures us that Jesus is still with us, seeking us out all the time. Letting him into our hearts is a daunting task for us. But this is something that Jesus is ready and wanting to do for us and in us. In fact, as Pope Francis asserts, Jesus has been waiting to shine his light through us, to guide us toward doing what he has called us to do. We just need to respond.

PONDER

Have I been really open to God's call?

PRAY

God of love and goodness, make me fearless in wanting to follow you, and keep me moving in the right direction.

11 | HOW TO BEST UNDERSTAND CHRIST'S LOVE

That same Jesus is now waiting for you to give him the chance to bring light to your life, to raise you up and to fill you with his strength.

Having spent the previous part of *Dilexit nos* discussing how Christ lived and worked among others, as related in the gospels, Pope Francis now turns more fully to one of the Church's favorite ways of expressing this love—the Sacred Heart of Jesus. By highlighting both the divinity and humanity of Jesus in this way, the Church reminds us of the part we are called to play in Jesus' work and of the strength that Jesus will give us to see it through.

PONDER
What does the image of the Sacred Heart mean to me?

PRAY
God of love and goodness, may the love that your heart shows me inspire me to follow your path.

12 | ACCEPTING THE GIFT

The image of the Sacred Heart also represents the inmost core of Jesus' Person.

Our heart is the organ that keeps our body functioning. It is the very core of our life. In the same way, Pope Francis says, the Sacred Heart of Jesus is the innermost core of his person. When we open ourselves to accept the gift of love that Jesus offers so freely and unconditionally, we will receive the strength and courage to do as he did. Will we perform great miracles of healing? Probably not, but we can perform the small personal miracles that a smile or kind word or a caring response can bring to someone who is in pain. The Sacred Heart of Jesus can show us the way to share Jesus' love everywhere.

PONDER

Am I ready to let Jesus' love work through me?

PRAY

God of love and goodness, let me be an expression of your love!

13 | THIS "ELOQUENT AND TANGIBLE SIGN"

The image of the Sacred Heart points us to the God who wished to become one of us, a part of our history, and a companion on our earthly journey.

Pope Francis points out that the popular image of the Sacred Heart does not isolate the heart from the totality of Jesus. We see Jesus looking directly at us and extending his hands toward us in welcome. His gesture is a very human one, one that we are able to imitate—reaching out to others with a direct gaze, being inclusive, and paying attention. Our relationship to Jesus is never abstract, but a personal encounter. He very much wants to be a part of our journey, and through the image of the Sacred Heart, he shows us how simple that encounter can be.

PONDER
How often am I truly involved in my interactions?

PRAY
God of love and goodness, help me to be as fearless and loving as you are with everyone I meet.

14 | WALKING THE WALK WITH JESUS

With the image of the Sacred Heart, we see how God willed to reveal himself and to draw close to us.

In this very pastoral and personal encyclical, Pope Francis wants us all to dedicate ourselves to following Jesus. In the image of the Sacred Heart, we see the enormity of Jesus' love expressed in terms we can easily emulate if we have the will to do so. But when we consider how fleeting most face-to-face encounters are these days (some only as close as a Zoom screen), it is easy, as the pope says, to race through them and miss the chance for real human contact. Ponder the image of seeing, not just looking; listening, not just hearing; and embracing, not just high-fiving. How different our encounters would be!

PONDER

How can I improve all my encounters?

PRAY

God of love and goodness, help me to seek depth instead of efficiency with everyone I meet.

15 | A HEART LIKE OURS

It is precisely in Jesus' human love, and not apart from it, that we encounter his divine love—"the infinite in the finite."

Pope Francis is eloquent when describing the depth of the heart of Christ. When his human love joins with his divine love, we begin to feel the power of his working within us. When we open ourselves to explore the depths of his heart, says the pope, we will find ourselves "overwhelmed by the immense glory of his infinite love." And it is the reality of knowing his human love that can open us to the divine love that will sustain and empower us.

PONDER
How have I experienced Christ's love?

PRAY
God of love and goodness, help me to feel your love always. May your love give me the will to be a more loving person!

16 | THROUGH, WITH, AND IN

Thanks to the prompting of the Spirit, our relationship with the heart of Christ is changed. We are led to the Father, the source of life...the ultimate wellspring of grace.

When we go to Mass, the Holy Spirit works through Jesus' loving heart to bring us to the Father. As Pope Francis reminds us, we always pray "through" Jesus, "with" Jesus, and "in" Jesus, who leads us to the Father, the source of all life and love.

And as the closing words of the Mass remind us, when we have been embraced by the love of Christ, we are not supposed to cling to it but to share it with others in the Spirit of love and hope.

PONDER

How do I understand the roles of each member of the Trinity in my quest to grow closer to God?

PRAY

God of love and goodness, guide my steps firmly and clearly so that I may always give you praise!

17 | THE FOUNT OF JESUS' LOVE

The pierced heart of Christ embodies all God's declarations of love present in the Scriptures.

Pope Francis next turns to the image of blood and water flowing from Jesus' side after he is pierced by the lance. This, he says, is the fount that saves God's people. For us, who know how the story turns out, this is indeed a healing and powerful image—Jesus literally giving his all to save us, right down to the last drop of his blood. Sacrifice on this level is hard to imagine, yet this is exactly what Jesus does to redeem us and make us a part of himself. The immensity of this gift should leave us in awe—and wondering at a love that is so deep.

PONDER
What is the biggest sacrifice I have ever made for a friend?

PRAY
God of love and goodness, open my heart to accept and appreciate your incredible gift to me.

18 | FROM GRIEF TO CONSOLATION

In contemplating the heart of Christ and his self-surrender, we ourselves can find great consolation.

Pope Francis says that contemplating Jesus' sacrifice should fill us with grief, but that's not where our response should stop. Instead, if we realize that Jesus' suffering unites him to all his disciples throughout time, our grief can turn to trust, to gratitude, and to peace. Most of us cannot hope to emulate Jesus' sacrifice in our lives, but we can sacrifice time or money or talents at the service of others—many of whom we may never meet. Jesus shares in the sufferings of all. By helping to heal Jesus' suffering in others, we come not only to share in that suffering but to find consolation in knowing we share in Christ's love.

PONDER

Have I experienced selflessly helping another? How can I make this part of my daily life?

PRAY

God of love and goodness, may I meet you always!

19 | RETURNING LOVE FOR LOVE

Our best response to the love of Christ's heart is to love our brothers and sisters. There is no greater way for us to return love for love.

"There is no greater way" to experience Jesus' love for us, says Pope Francis, than by returning "love for love." He goes on to say that the Scriptures are the only guide we need to understand how Jesus wants us to act—always at the service of others, just as he offered his life for us. The image of his Sacred Heart welcomes us into the depth of his suffering but also into the joy and consolation of that sacrifice. It is a profound mystery and awe-inspiring in its simplicity. We are all capable of responding.

PONDER
Do I sometimes (consciously or not) complicate the simple messages God is offering me?

PRAY
God of love and goodness, help me to serve you in simplicity instead of complexity!

20 | STREAMS OF LIVING WATER

Jesus displays his glory in and through our littleness.

In addition to devotion to the Sacred Heart, the Church venerates the Immaculate Heart of Mary, whose unique mediation with God is so important. But that's not all. The opening in Jesus' side, Pope Francis says, is expansive enough to include Mary and all believers, making us all "streams of living water," integral and necessary parts of Jesus' heart and message to the world. Such all-inclusive love is God's great gift. No matter how insignificant we seem, God considers each of us eminently worthy of care, attention, and love, and God wants us to help bring that care, attention, and love to everyone.

PONDER

Does someone I know need to hear today that they are worthy of God's love?

PRAY

God of love and goodness, let all my actions reflect your love!

21 | A NEW CIVILIZATION OF LOVE

Good intentions are not enough. An outward action has to give expression to an inward desire.

It is one thing to be moved by the Sacred Heart to want to make things better, but that desire needs to be accompanied by action on our part. Is there something we can do in our homes, workplaces, parishes, and neighborhoods that will improve the living conditions or quality of life for those around us? And how do we begin to take action against the injustices in our society? Pope Francis says that, for Christians immersed in Christ's love, it has to begin with two challenging tasks: acknowledging our own guilt and asking forgiveness.

PONDER

How hard or easy would it be for me to help?

PRAY

God of love and goodness, help me to see where your healing touch is needed—and to reach out!

22 | SEEKING FORGIVENESS IS THE FIRST STEP

Asking forgiveness is a means of healing relationships, for it "re-opens dialogue and manifests the will to re-establish the bond of fraternal charity."

Pope Francis is clear that responding to Jesus' call to share the love of the Sacred Heart begins with asking forgiveness. We may no longer be able to heal some rifts, but in asking forgiveness when we can, we can reduce someone's hurt. To ask forgiveness sincerely is to make ourselves vulnerable as Jesus did. This vulnerability is not a sign of weakness but of courage and strength—it costs a lot to stand humbly before another and confess fault, but it is the only way to begin.

PONDER

How good am I at sincerely asking forgiveness?

PRAY

God of love and goodness, fill me with the desire both to freely seek and freely give forgiveness!

23 | HEALING THE WOUNDS OF THE CHURCH AND THE WORLD

By practicing reparation, we offer the healing power of the heart of Christ new ways of expressing itself.

Pope Francis says that when we actively make amends for the wrongs we have done, we carry Jesus' love to people who have known not love but injustice and rejection. Those in 12-step groups are familiar with the concept of making amends to those who have been hurt by our actions. Adopting this principle in our everyday life can begin to make a huge difference in beginning to heal our broken world.

PONDER
How easy is it for me to say "please forgive me"?

PRAY
God of love and goodness, fill my heart with compassion so that I may learn to share your love!

24 | HUMILITY AND CLOSENESS

Once our hearts welcome Jesus' love in complete trust, and enable its fire to spread in our lives, we become capable of loving others as Christ did.

Even in our smallest acts of reaching out in compassion to others, Pope Francis assures us that we are actively sharing the love of Christ. Christ humbles himself, the pope reminds us, to use our love to bring his love to those who are hungry for it. No action is too small if it is done with the intention of bringing Jesus' light and love to others. In this way, Jesus enables us to love as he loved and to bring his love to our fragmented world.

PONDER

Do I ever think of myself as sharing God's love?

PRAY

God of love and goodness, may your love burn so brightly inside me that I have no choice but to share it!

25 | SHARING IN THE PASCHAL MYSTERY

The risen Lord, by the working of his grace, mysteriously unites us to his passion.

Pope Francis wants us to understand the enormity of what we are doing when we seek to share in the Sacred Heart of Jesus. This is no less than joining Jesus in his paschal mystery—we join our sufferings to his and thereby take part in his singular act of redemption. More than this, we are also joined to the Father through the Spirit, making our choice a true participation in God's Trinity! And all we have to do to share in this gift is to say "yes."

PONDER

Have I truly grasped what this participation in Jesus' heart means?

PRAY

God of love and goodness, make me worthy to serve you always!

26 | A MISSION OF LOVE

*As we contemplate the Sacred Heart,
mission becomes a matter of love.*

The greatest danger in accepting the mission of following the Sacred Heart, says Pope Francis, is that, with all that we say and do, we may fail to display the most important element—a joyful encounter with the love of Christ. If what we do in Jesus' name becomes a chore instead of a true reaching out in love, we are not connecting with the Sacred Heart, who embraces us and saves us. When we let this sanctifying love fill us first, we will have a joyful abundance to give away.

PONDER
How often am I suffused with joy when trying to act as Jesus would?

PRAY
God of love and goodness, let me feel your love always so that I may share it as you do!

27 | MISSION—MORE THAN "ME AND JESUS"

Love for the brothers and sisters of our communities—religious, parochial, diocesan, and others—is a kind of fuel that feeds our friendship with Jesus.

Remember the words of Jesus: "By this everyone will know that you are my disciples, if you have love for one another." True mission does not happen without community. Indeed, the pope asserts, showing love for others may be the only way we can truly manifest this love. Our love for others, starting at home and reaching out to include our parish, our neighborhood, our diocese, and the entire Church and world is what fuels our mission to follow Jesus and to continue to share his love everywhere.

PONDER

How widely do I experience community?

PRAY

God of love and goodness, give me the grace to find you everywhere.

28 | WHAT YOU DID FOR THE LEAST OF THESE...

Jesus asks that you meet him in every one of our brothers and sisters. What a beautiful encounter that can be!

When we encounter others as we seek to follow the will of God, says Pope Francis, we have to remember that some of those "others" will be people whom society deems unacceptable or despised. These, too, he reminds us, are our brothers and sisters. The Sacred Heart of Jesus lives in everyone. Our hearts will expand if we are open to meeting Jesus in everyone we meet. Meeting Christ in unexpected people and places can lead us into the beautiful heart of Christ's love.

PONDER
Do I find Jesus in everyone I meet?

PRAY
God of love and goodness, let me not shrink from any encounter where I might meet you!

29 | YOU ARE NOT ALONE

Jesus is calling you to spread goodness in our world. This is a call of service, a summons to do good.

Whatever our vocation in life—married, single, parent, and whatever profession or job we do—Pope Francis says that if we are responding to Jesus' call, then we are making his Sacred Heart alive in our world. It's not always easy to keep our spirits up, but Pope Francis says that we can rely on the fact that we'll never be alone—Jesus will always be with us to strengthen, inspire, and encourage us.

PONDER
How often do I remember that I am doing Jesus' work?

PRAY
God of love and goodness, help me to remember that everything I do is in your name!

30 | ENTIRELY A MATTER OF THE HEART

Only the heart is capable of setting us in a place of reverence and loving obedience before the Lord.

If we pursue our daily duties out of a sense of self-interest, we will miss the great opportunity of getting to know God better, of opening ourselves to God's love, and of sharing that love in all we do. Pope Francis urges us to take the Sacred Heart as a guide for how to love. When our mind is enlightened by the Spirit, our heart is able to open to the simple (but not easy) call that Jesus makes to us. It is all a matter of the heart, Pope Francis says. Let us take the beautiful step of joining our hearts to his and working to change the world!

PONDER
What do I need to do to make a genuine beginning to living a life of love in Jesus' name?

PRAY
God of love and goodness, help me to serve all people with a fullness of love and grace!